PROTECTING EARTH'S
AIR
QUALITY

VALERIE RAPP

LERNER PUBLICATIONS COMPANY · MINNEAPOLIS

This book is dedicated to children with asthma. My hope is that the world finds a way to heal their lungs and give them healthy air, so they may know the joy of breathing deeply and freely.

Text copyright © 2009 by Valerie Rapp

Lerner Publications Company
A division of Lerner Publishing Group, Inc.
241 First Avenue North
Minneapolis, MN 55401 U.S.A.

Website address: www.lernerbooks.com

Library of Congress Cataloging-in-Publication Data

Rapp, Valerie.
        Protecting Earth's air quality / by Valerie Rapp.
            p.   cm. — (Saving our living earth)
        Includes bibliographical references and index.
        ISBN 978-0-8225-7558-0 (lib. bdg. : alk. paper)
        1. Air—Pollution—Juvenile literature. 2. Air quality management—Juvenile literature.
    I. Title.
    TD883.13.R37 2009
    363.739′2—dc22   2008000907

Manufactured in the United States of America
1 2 3 4 5 6 — DP — 14 13 12 11 10 09

CONTENTS

INTRODUCTION

Steam rising from nearby roofs disappears into the sky. A crow on a tree branch flaps its wings and lifts off into the air. Above the crow, clouds move across the sky. Smoke from distant smokestacks rises into the clouds. Far, far above us, planes cross the sky, carrying people to other cities.

The air we exhale mixes with the air outside. The air we inhale into our lungs smells like the roses blooming nearby, freshly cut grass, or the exhaust pumping out of car tailpipes. That's how we can tell where the air has been before we breathed it.

Above: The air we breathe carries the scent of wherever the air just came from. Air can smell like flowers or *(right)* like car exhaust.
Facing page: Smoke and steam pump out of these smokestacks.

What is this air that we breathe every moment, walk through every day, and hardly think about most of the time? Because air can't usually be seen, scientists have found it harder to study air than almost anything else. For a long time, scientists knew more about the stars, dinosaurs, and oceans than they knew about air. But they did know that people and all animals need air to stay alive. Through experiments, scientists discovered that air is a mixture of gases and learned how our bodies and how plants use air.

When the air gets dirty—what scientists call air pollution—it makes people cough and hurts their lungs. Dirty air also kills trees and other plants too. People have cleaned up lots of air pollution already, but more needs to be done. Luckily, there are lots of things we can all do to help clean up air pollution.

People have cleaned up lots of air pollution already, but more needs to be done.

CHAPTER ONE

THE INVISIBLE OCEAN OF AIR

Take a deep breath. Now breathe out—and in again. Most of the time, we hardly think about breathing. But we need air every second of our lives. If you've ever held your breath underwater, you know that you can't go very long without fresh air.

We all share the air. When we exhale, our breath mixes back into the air. Before long, the kid next to you is breathing in some of the air that you breathed out. Not only that, but you breathe in air that others breathed out. So if you're playing with your dog, you're pulling into your lungs air that your dog breathed out not long ago.

Anything that goes into the air travels with the air. Good smells, like sizzling hamburgers, are carried along, and so are bad smells, like car exhaust. Pollution in the air reaches our noses, and we breathe it into our lungs. Some air pollution smells bad, but much air pollution has no smell at all.

Air pollution can make people sick. To find out how air affects us and why it's important to keep air clean, we need to know more about what makes up the air we breathe.

Anything that goes into the air travels with the air.

Facing page: This girl and her dog are sharing more than a hug—they breathe the same air too. *Below:* Smog sits over the city of Santiago, Chile, in 2007. The Chilean capital is one of the most polluted cities in South America.

WHAT'S IN THE AIR WE BREATHE?

The air is made up of a mixture of gases. To breathe, human beings and all animals need just one gas—oxygen. But about 78 percent of the air is made of nitrogen gas. Oxygen is about one-fifth, or 21 percent, of the air. (If the air were pure oxygen, we would all be on fire. Pure oxygen burns very easily.)

All the other gases besides nitrogen and oxygen make up about 1 percent of the air. They are still important even though they make up such a small percentage. These gases include argon, carbon dioxide, neon, helium, methane, krypton, nitrous oxide, hydrogen, xenon, and ozone. The mixture of gases stays mainly the same all through the atmosphere—the layers of air surrounding Earth.

Imagine the gases in the air as colorful balloons filling a room. Each atom of gas would be one balloon. If the room had exactly one hundred balloons, here's how many balloons of each gas would be in the room:

Nitrogen	78 balloons
Oxygen	21 balloons
Argon	90 percent of a single balloon
All the other gases	10 percent of a single balloon

VERY, VERY SMALL PARTICLES

All matter—that includes solid objects, liquids, and gases in the air—is made up of very tiny particles called molecules. Molecules are so small that people can see them only by using a special microscope. Molecules are groups of even smaller particles called atoms.

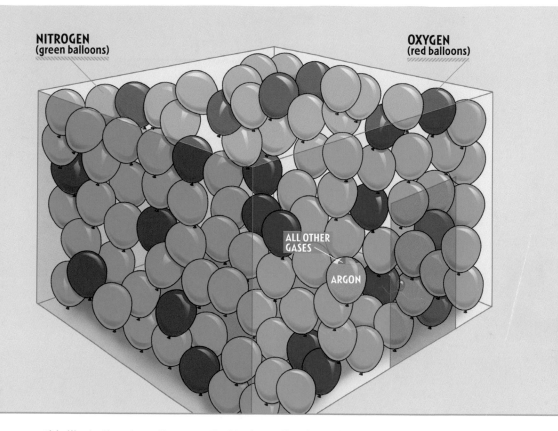

ALL OTHER GASES

ARGON

This illustration shows the gases that make up the atmosphere. Balloons are used to signify the different gases.

Our lungs pull oxygen from the air. The oxygen enters our blood and is carried throughout our entire body. Muscles use oxygen to move, and brains use oxygen to think.

As our body uses oxygen, it creates carbon dioxide. Blood carries carbon dioxide back to our lungs. When we breathe out, we send carbon dioxide out into the air.

Plants can't live without carbon dioxide, just as animals can't live without oxygen. Plants take in carbon dioxide and sunlight from the air. They pull up water through their roots. Using energy from sunlight, plants turn the carbon

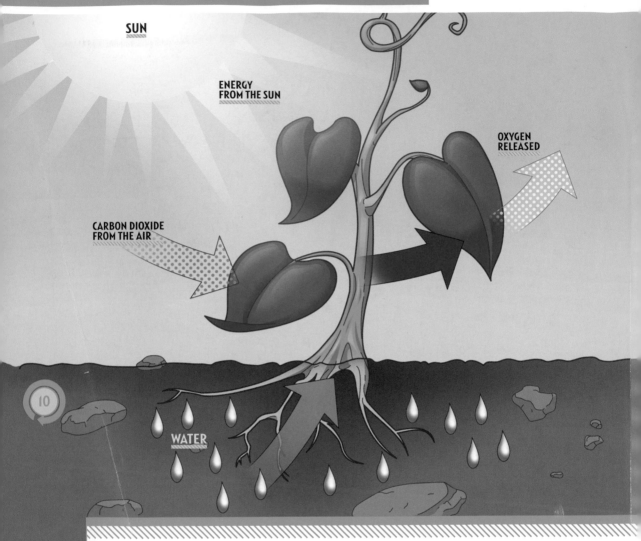

SUN

ENERGY FROM THE SUN

OXYGEN RELEASED

CARBON DIOXIDE FROM THE AIR

10

WATER

In a process called photosynthesis, plants use energy from the sun to convert carbon dioxide and water into food. They release oxygen into the air.

dioxide and water into food. In this process, called photosynthesis, plants release the oxygen, a gas that's part of carbon dioxide, back into the air. We can see this in aquariums, when we see bubbles of oxygen rising from the underwater plants. Plants on land also release oxygen into the air. Just two healthy trees make enough oxygen to meet one person's needs on a daily basis.

OUR ATMOSPHERE

On a sunny day, the blue sky seems to go on forever. Much of what you are seeing in the sky is part of Earth's atmosphere. The word *atmo* means "vapor" in Greek, and the word *sphere* means "ball" or "globe." The oxygen we breathe is part of the ball of air that circles our planet. We are walking around at the bottom of an invisible ocean of air.

The atmosphere is made up of four layers. Closest to the ground is the troposphere (lower atmosphere). It is about 10 miles (16 kilometers) deep. Most clouds and weather are in this layer. Next is the stratosphere (upper atmosphere), which reaches from the top of the troposphere to about 30 miles (48 km) above Earth. These two layers have the most effect on people and other living things. When we

CAN YOU KEEP PAPER DRY WHEN IT'S UNDERWATER?

Here's an easy way to see that air is real, even though it's invisible. Do this experiment in a sink or outside.

<u>What you'll need:</u> A clear glass, one sheet of scrap paper, and a bowl taller than the glass. A clear bowl works best. Food coloring can make the experiment more fun.

Fill the bowl with water, and add food coloring if you have some. Crumple the scrap paper and push it into the bottom of the glass. With the glass upside down, push it straight down in the bowl. Don't let go! After a few seconds, pull the glass out and see if the paper is wet.

(Based on an experiment in David Suzuki and Kathy Vanderlinden's *Eco-Fun: Great Projects, Experiments, and Games for a Greener Earth.* Vancouver, BC: Douglas & McIntyre Publishing Group, Greystone Books, 2001.)

talk about cleaning up dirty air, we are talking about the air in these two layers.

The atmosphere contains the oxygen we need. It also preserves life in other ways. The gases in the atmosphere let sunlight pass through to the ground. Sunlight provides the energy that fuels life. It supplies the energy that green plants use to grow.

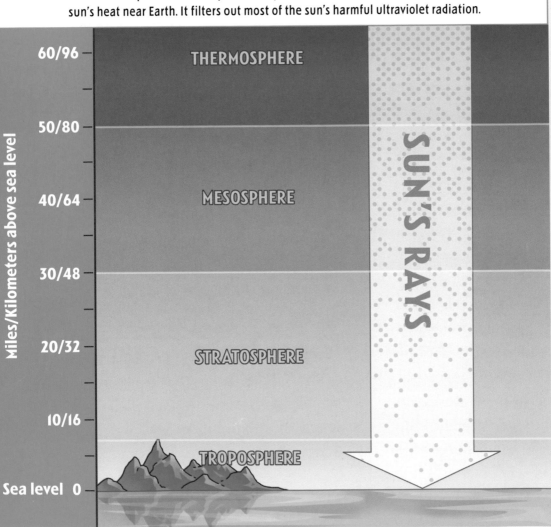

Earth's atmosphere is made up of four layers. The atmosphere keeps some of the sun's heat near Earth. It filters out most of the sun's harmful ultraviolet radiation.

Sunlight also provides the heat that makes Earth warmer than outer space. Our atmosphere absorbs some of the sun's heat and keeps it near the ground, somewhat like a space blanket. Because of the atmosphere, Earth is just warm enough for life to exist. But it's not so hot that water boils away into steam.

Even though the atmosphere lets sunlight through, it blocks most of the sun's harmful rays from reaching Earth. These harmful rays are in the form of ultraviolet radiation. Although we can see sunlight, we can't see ultraviolet radiation. We can feel it though! Ultraviolet radiation causes sunburn.

ON THE EDGE OF SPACE

Up, up, up—but not away! Gravity is the force that keeps objects on the ground. It also pulls air molecules toward the ground, keeping most of the air within 18 miles (30 km) of the ground. Above that the air gets thinner and thinner until it is hard to tell where the atmosphere ends and outer space begins.

Within the stratosphere, a very thin layer of gas absorbs most ultraviolet radiation. This is called the ozone layer. The ozone layer has only one gas—ozone. Ozone is a gas made up of three oxygen atoms. An atom is the tiniest part of an element. Without the ozone layer, ultraviolet radiation would be hundreds of times stronger. People would get skin cancer more easily. Green plants would struggle to grow under the harsh radiation.

Because air is made up of gases, air is able to seep into the ground under our feet. Earthworms and other tiny animals underground breathe from the tiny amounts of air found among particles of dirt. Air is also mixed into bodies of

Fish, like this goldfish, use their gills to breathe underwater.

water such as lakes, rivers, and oceans. Underwater, fish use their gills to filter oxygen from water in order to breathe. Diving spiders don't have gills, so they carry air bubbles down with them. They breathe from these air bubbles while they swim underwater.

CARBON IN MOTION

All life, including people and plants, needs carbon. Carbon, a chemical element, is the basic building block of life. From the smallest insect to the largest whale, from the tiniest flower to the biggest tree, everything that's alive has carbon.

Carbon can change from a gas to a solid and back to a gas again. Plants get their carbon from carbon dioxide. In making food in photosynthesis, plants use carbon dioxide and turn it into solid carbon, a part of the plant. Humans and other animals get carbon by eating plants (and eating animals that ate plants). Carbon is an element in all our food. It

14

HOW MUCH AIR DO YOU NEED?

The more active we are, the more oxygen we need. When we run or work hard, we breathe hard to get more air into our lungs. The average person needs about 2 gallons (7.5 liters) of air per minute when lying down, 4 gallons (15 liters) per minute when reading a book, and 12 gallons (45 liters) per minute or more when running.

THE CARBON CYCLE

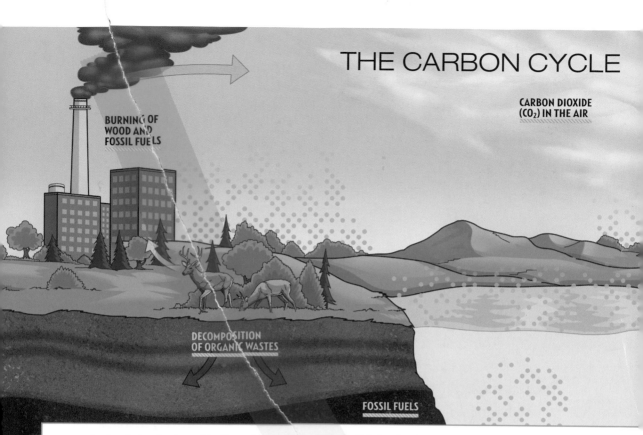

CARBON DIOXIDE (CO₂) IN THE AIR

BURNING OF WOOD AND FOSSIL FUELS

DECOMPOSITION OF ORGANIC WASTES

FOSSIL FUELS

Carbon is in plants and in the animals that eat them. It is in plant and animal matter that decomposes, or breaks down, in the ground. Carbon is released into the air as a gas when animals breathe out or when fossil fuels are burned.

becomes part of our bones, muscles, blood, brain, heart—our whole bodies. Our bodies turn some carbon back into gas, which we breathe out as carbon dioxide.

When trees and plants die, bacteria and fungi in the soil break the wood, stems, and leaves back into simpler forms, including carbon dioxide. The natural process of decay puts carbon dioxide back into the air. Then plants can draw it in again. So all of life keeps carbon moving.

People and plants exchange oxygen and carbon dioxide all the time. They each put into the air exactly what the other one needs. Life wouldn't be able to keep going without carbon changing form. Scientists call this process the carbon cycle.

This ice core was drilled from Anarctica in 1993. A glaciologist, a scientist who studies glaciers, is taking the ice core out to study the bubbles trapped in the ice.

16

Hundreds of millions of years ago, the atmosphere had more carbon dioxide and less oxygen than it does in modern times. Early forms of life began to pull carbon dioxide out of the air, using the carbon and putting oxygen back into the air.

These early life-forms included tiny sea creatures that lived in the world's oceans. As they died, they drifted to the ocean bottom and slowly piled up in deep layers. In shallow swamps, plants lived, died, and built up in thick layers.

HOW SCIENTISTS FIND "OLD AIR"

Scientists study air bubbles that get trapped in ice. Old ice has bubbles of old air frozen inside it. So to learn the history of air, scientists drilled into the oldest ice on Earth—the ice sheets of Greenland and Antarctica. They drilled up to 6,562 feet (2,000 meters) deep within the thick ice to cut out ice cores.

Scientists learned that the level of carbon dioxide began rising in the atmosphere soon after the Industrial Revolution began in the 1700s. Carbon dioxide levels are now higher than they were at any other time in the last 160,000 years.

Over many millions of years, all those layers of dead sea creatures and swamp plants built up as forms of stored carbon. They turned into what we call fossil fuels. Fossil fuels include oil, coal, and natural gas. Because these layers built up so long ago, the fossil fuels are underground or even under the ocean floor.

While carbon was being stored underground in fossil fuels, oxygen was being released into the air. The mixture of gases in the atmosphere began to change. Finally, the atmosphere had the amount of oxygen that made life on Earth as we know it possible.

THE BEGINNING OF FOSSIL FUELS

Almost 80 percent of the world's energy comes from fossil fuels. Most of the fossil fuels formed before the dinosaurs lived.

Coal is loaded into a truck in a mine in Australia.

CHAPTER TWO

HOW AIR CAN MAKE US SICK

Modern life is exciting. Cars and buses fill busy city streets. Our homes shine with bright lights. Airplanes carry us to and from places. It takes a huge amount of energy to keep the lights on, the cars moving, and to produce all the things that people use every day. However, our modern world and the energy it uses create air pollution.

The World Health Organization (WHO) says that air pollution causes 3 million deaths worldwide every year. That's three times the number of people who die from traffic accidents. Millions more people get sick because of polluted air but don't die.

The WHO says that air pollution causes 3 million deaths worldwide every year.

Different types of air pollution make people sick. Smoke, soot, and other tiny particles in the air are the worst air pollution problem. A second problem is dangerous gases created when fossil fuels are used. These unhealthy gases spread through the air that we all breathe. Other air pollution problems don't make people sick but cause certain problems in our atmosphere.

Air pollution can happen indoors too. Smoke and soot are the biggest air pollution problem indoors as well as outdoors

Facing page: A worker in Hong Kong, China, has a towel wrapped around his face to protect him from air pollution. *Below:* Huge columns of smoke from forest fires can cause air pollution hundreds of miles away.

SMOKE GETS IN YOUR LUNGS

The most dangerous air pollution problem is the one we've known about the longest—particle pollution. When objects such as wood and coal burn, tiny pieces, or particles, of carbon enter the air as smoke and soot. Smoke, soot, and exhaust from cars and trucks all carry small particles, and these particles are especially bad for us.

Smoke and soot were obvious problems since the first time somebody coughed around a campfire. We start coughing when we breathe smoke because our bodies are trying to get rid of the harmful particles. But not even our coughing can get all the particles out.

Our bodies can filter out large particles. But very small particles get deep into our lungs. They get all the way to the tiny air sacs where oxygen is absorbed into the body. For this reason, the very small particles are the ones that are the most dangerous. They can

THE INDUSTRIAL REVOLUTION

The Industrial Revolution began in the late-1700s in Great Britain. This was the start of air pollution far worse than people had ever known. The Industrial Revolution introduced many new machines to a range of industries. Because of this, people started to burn lots of coal. Coal ran the steam engines that powered factories, and coal heated homes in growing cities. Coal smoke and soot began to fill city air. During London's winter fogs, the coal smoke was trapped near the ground for days. London became famous for its "pea-soup fogs" in the 1800s. People could hardly see ahead of themselves as they walked city streets.

20

cause the most harm to our health.

These small particles are described by their diameter, measured in microns. Particles 10 microns (4/10,000ths of an inch) or less in diameter are a health concern. Particles 2.5 microns (1/10,000th of an inch) or less in diameter are the most dangerous.

Particles damage the lungs' ability to absorb oxygen. They lead to infections and other lung diseases. Over time, these very small particles can cause lung cancer. Smoke and soot particles are especially bad for anyone with asthma. Asthma is a disease that narrows airways in the lungs and causes breathing problems. Children's growing lungs and older people's weaker lungs are affected the most by particle pollution.

Volcanic eruptions are a natural source of particle pollution. Krakatoa, a volcano off the coast of Indonesia, erupted in 1883. It destroyed most of an island and threw billions of tons of dust into the atmosphere. Volcanic

HOW SMALL IS 2.5 MICRONS?

A single human hair is about 60 microns, or 24/10,000ths of an inch, thick. A row of six 10-micron particles could fit on the tip of a human hair. Thirty of the 2.5-micron particles most dangerous to our lungs could fit on the tip of a human hair.

21

Krakatoa volcano in Indonesia erupted in 1883. Since then the volcano has regrown (shown here in 1995) and was renamed Anak-Krakatoa, meaning "son of Krakatoa."

dust circled the world within two weeks. For more than a year, the thick clouds of volcanic dust kept weather cooler around the world.

Forest fires are another natural source of particle pollution. The massive smoke columns from large forest fires look like huge thunderclouds rising into the sky. Forest fire smoke can travel hundreds of miles. From 1997 to 1998, large forest fires in Southeast Asia caused lung infections to increase in several countries. People in Malaysia and the island of Sumatra went to doctors for coughs, infections, and breathing problems caused by the smoke.

These large fires burned in Indonesia in Southeast Asia for weeks. Constant smoke in the air made people sick, even though they were many miles away.

BLOWING IN THE WIND

The soot and smoke from fossil fuels are fairly easy to see. But scientists also began to realize that the smoke included dangerous gases that affect people's health. These gases are invisible and hard to detect.

Sulfur dioxide, nitrogen oxides, and carbon monoxide are three of these gases. *Oxide* means the gases include oxygen, but the oxygen is combined with another element. Sulfur dioxide combines sulfur and oxygen. Nitrogen oxides combine nitrogen and oxygen. And carbon monoxide combines carbon and oxygen.

These three gases all come from burning fossil fuels. Most of the sulfur dioxide comes from power plants that burn coal. It also comes from other large sources such as paper mills and chemical plants. Nitrogen oxides are produced by cars, trucks, and other motor vehicles, as well as by some power plants and factories. The third gas, carbon monoxide, is produced from burning fossil fuels too. It is also produced when wood and paper are burned, whether in forest fires or wood stoves.

Since air is made up of gases, it is always moving. Every time we feel a breeze, we are feeling air in motion. Air pollutants such as carbon monoxide travel everywhere that air goes, which is all around the world. Local winds blow air pollution to the neighbor's house or over to the next town. Jet streams carry air pollution for hundreds of miles.

SOME IS GOOD BUT MORE IS TOO MUCH!

Plants need nitrogen to grow, and humans need it to build substances in our cells called proteins and to have strong bones. But too much nitrogen can end up in the air near cities and farms. Then it adds to acid rain and smog.

23

The soot and smoke from this factory smokestack are easy to see. But air pollution also includes gases we can't see that are bad for our health.

Jet streams are fast-moving rivers of air high in the sky. They move at 60 to 250 miles (96 to 402 km) per hour, at a height of 8 to 12 miles (13 to 19 km) above the ground. Jet streams curve and shift as the weather changes. But their general direction is always from west to east. Each of the major jet streams can be several hundred miles across and up to 2 miles (3 km) deep. Once air pollution reaches the jet streams, the jet streams carry it to other countries and even across oceans.

Sometimes air *doesn't* move very much, like when cold air gets trapped in a valley. Cold air doesn't rise, so it stays there. Then the pollution gets trapped close to the ground. It can become so thick that people get sick just by breathing.

WHEN GOOD RAIN GOES BAD

Rain is the sky's way of cleaning the air. Sulfur dioxide, nitrogen dioxide, dust, soot, and other pollutants are washed out of the sky when it rains. But the pollutants make the rain more acidic than usual.

Acid rain is any water from the sky—rain, sleet, snow, or fog drip—that contains chemical pollutants. It's not so acidic that it burns people. But acid rain harms plants. Coal-burning power plants and some factories make smoke that causes acid rain. Places near the factories have the worst acid rain. Sometimes it's bad enough that fish die in the lakes.

Mercury, a toxic metal, is a pollutant found in smoke from coal-burning power plants. Rain can drop mercury into rivers and lakes, where fish swallow it.

25

Coal-burning power plants and some factories make smoke that causes acid rain.

Many states have had to warn people not to eat fish from certain lakes because the mercury levels are dangerously high. Most fish are still safe to eat, but people need to heed warning signs posted on fishing lakes.

SMOG AND OZONE

In the 1950s, yellow or brown haze began to appear in some of the world's largest cities. The brownish haze is called smog. It was especially common in Los Angeles, California, known for its heavy traffic.

Smog turned out to be more than just all the car exhaust smearing the sky. When sunlight hits the nitrogen oxides and other pollutants in the air, the light breaks apart the chemicals. It changes them into other chemicals. More light creates more smog, so sunny days have the worst smog.

One of the most common chemicals in smog is ozone. Ozone has been around for millions of years—in the upper atmosphere. Up there, miles above

26

A cloud of thick smog hangs over downtown Los Angeles, California. The city has had problems with air pollution since the 1950s.

the ground, the ozone layer shields us from much of the sun's ultraviolet radiation. But the ozone near the ground, scientists found, makes people cough and sets off asthma attacks. Smog damages plants too, such as farm crops and trees.

In fact, air pollution threatens mountain forests in many places around the world. Ozone, sulfur dioxide, and nitrogen oxides drifting up from cities damage trees. Tree leaves and needles begin to drop. Over time, trees weaken and are more likely to die. As the pollutants settle out of the air, they can poison soil and streams.

IS OZONE GOOD OR BAD?

Ground-level ozone is bad for us. It makes us cough and makes our eyes water. The ozone layer in the upper atmosphere protects us from too much ultraviolet radiation. You can remember this with this little jingle: "Ozone nearby, bad for you and I. Ozone up high, good in the sky." Ground-level ozone that is part of smog does not rise all the way to the upper atmosphere, where the ozone layer is. So it is no help in fixing the ozone layer.

The ozone layer in the upper atmosphere is affected by chlorofluorocarbons (CFCs). CFCs are a group of human-made gas mixtures that include carbon, chlorine, fluorine, and other gases. Starting in the 1930s, CFCs were used in refrigerators and air conditioners to create a cooling effect. They were also used in spray cans to make them spray. The CFCs leaked into the air first when these products were made. They leaked again when these products were thrown out and smashed with other garbage.

Scientists discovered that CFCs in the air reached the ozone layer in the upper atmosphere. They were destroying the ozone layer. As holes opened up in the ozone layer, more ultraviolet radiation from the sun could reach the ground. More ultraviolet radiation increases the risk of skin cancer. It also damages eyes and ages skin faster.

TURNING UP THE HEAT: GREENHOUSE GASES

You know how dangerous it is to sit in a parked car with the windows closed on a hot day. The windows let sunlight in but don't let heat escape. The heat gets unbearable in just a few minutes.

Just as car windows trap heat inside a car, our atmosphere traps the sun's heat near Earth. Certain gases in the atmosphere absorb some of the sun's heat and send it back to Earth. These "greenhouse gases" include carbon dioxide, methane, nitrous oxide, and others. They keep Earth warm in the same way a greenhouse keeps its plants warm. Without this natural greenhouse effect, Earth would be about 60°F (15°C) colder, making it a planet of ice.

Since the beginning of the Industrial Revolution, people have been adding more greenhouse gases to the atmosphere, far beyond the natural amounts that have long been there. Greenhouse gases are in the smoke from factories and power plants and the exhaust from cars and trucks. Since the 1800s, the carbon dioxide level has been slowly rising worldwide. It is now about one-third higher than it was in the mid-1800s.

We still have plenty of oxygen to breathe. But the rising level of greenhouse gases appears to be causing global warming. When scientists refer to "global warming," they don't mean just hot weather. They are talking about climate change.

Climate is the long-term patterns of weather, like ice ages coming and going. Most scientists agree that Earth's climate has been getting warmer over the past twenty years. This is mainly because greenhouse gases are trapping more heat in

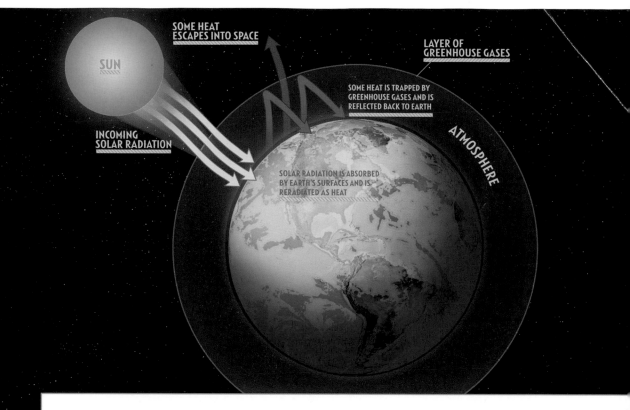

SUN

INCOMING
SOLAR RADIATION

SOME HEAT
ESCAPES INTO SPACE

LAYER OF
GREENHOUSE GASES

SOME HEAT IS TRAPPED BY
GREENHOUSE GASES AND IS
REFLECTED BACK TO EARTH

ATMOSPHERE

SOLAR RADIATION IS ABSORBED
BY EARTH'S SURFACES AND IS
RERADIATED AS HEAT

Carbon dioxide and other greenhouse gases in the atmosphere trap some of the
sun's heat near Earth. This is called the greenhouse effect.

the atmosphere. As long as the level of greenhouse gases stays high, the climate
will keep getting warmer.

INDOOR AIR POLLUTION

Air is everywhere and, unfortunately, so is air pollution. It's even indoors. Not only
does smoke and dust drift in from outside, some air pollution problems start indoors.

More than half of the world's 6.6 billion people use wood, coal, or even animal
dung to cook meals and heat their homes. Because they are poor, most of these
people don't have good chimneys or vents to take the smoke outside. The
indoor smoke causes lung infections and even pneumonia.

According to the World Health Organization, indoor smoke kills about 1.6 million people around the world every year. It especially affects women, who do most of the cooking, and children under five years old, who are indoors with their mothers.

The best way to prevent indoor smoke is to switch to cleaner fuels, such as solar energy, gas, or electricity. Also, people need better stoves and houses with vents or fans that carry the smoke outside.

A personal form of indoor air pollution that we can control is cigarette smoke. Tobacco smoke has more than four thousand chemicals, including the poisons arsenic and cyanide. Smoking tobacco is like taking air pollution out of a smokestack and sucking it directly into your lungs. The nicotine in tobacco is addictive, making it hard to stop smoking.

The WHO figures that every year, about five million people die from illnesses caused by tobacco. Smokers have more trouble with all kinds of lung infections. Years of smoking can lead to cancer. However, the risk of cancer goes down fast after a person quits smoking.

Tobacco smoke can affect everyone. Secondhand smoke drifts in the air around smokers. Recent studies have shown that secondhand smoke makes both smokers and nonsmokers sick.

Smoke isn't the only kind of indoor air pollution. Mold and the fumes from household cleaners and insect sprays can all be harmful to people's lungs. People can be safe by not breathing these fumes. Most common molds can be cleaned up easily. A few kinds of mold must be cleaned up by experts.

CLEARING THE AIR

We don't necessarily have to give up our modern lifestyles to solve air pollution. Over the past thirty years, the United States, Canada, and European countries have cleaned up some of their air pollution problems. In fact, levels of the worst air pollutants have declined 35 to 70 percent from their highest levels. That means in many parts of these countries, kids are breathing cleaner air than their grandparents breathed when they were young.

Not every country has the same story, however. Many countries around the world have serious air pollution problems. Even in the countries that have made progress, lots of pollution still goes into the air. As we have seen, air pollution from a factory travels on the wind. And the wind blows all the way around the world.

EXPERIMENT: TEST FOR PARTICLES IN YOUR NEIGHBORHOOD

You can collect data on particles in the air around your home and neighborhood.

What you'll need: Several 5- by 8-inch (13- by 20-centimeters) index cards, scissors, clear packaging tape, a hole punch, and string or twist ties.

Label each card with the date and place where you plan to hang it. In the center of each card, cut out a rectangle 1 inch (2.5 cm) wide and 3 inches (7.6 cm) long. Place a strip of clear packaging tape over the cutout. The sticky tape showing through the cutout is your particle collector. Punch a hole at the top of the card.

Use string or twist ties to hang cards at different places outside. (Make sure you have permission!) Hang at least one card near a road or parking lot and another card from a tree. Hang one card inside your house or classroom.

After one week, collect the cards and look at the particles stuck on the tape.

Tip: Put each card on top of a sheet of white paper for contrast. Use a magnifying glass or microscope to see smaller particles.

CHAPTER THREE

CHANGE IS IN THE AIR

People are doing something about air pollution! In many countries, lawmakers have passed laws that make factories and power plants clean up their smoke. They have also passed laws to reduce the pollution coming from cars, buses, and trucks. All around the world, families, schools, and towns are finding ways they can fight air pollution too.

These actions can make a difference. Cleaner air can save millions of lives. All of us would be able to breathe easier. Although some air pollution problems are scary, they aren't impossible to solve.

Cleaner air can save millions of lives.

WINDS OF CHANGE

Long before modern times, King Edward I (1239-1307) of England banned the burning of sea coal. Sea coal released foul smoke into the London air. This ban from more than seven hundred years ago was the first known law to fight air pollution.

During the Industrial Revolution, coal smoke and soot filled city air in Great Britain. In the late 1800s, British doctors and other citizens worked to pass laws that made factories control their pollution. But the factory owners fought the new laws, and the courts threw out these early laws. Besides, at that time, factory owners didn't really know how to control their smoke except by shutting down factories. For all these reasons, factories and power plants kept pouring smoke into the air.

Cars line up on a road in Beijing, China, while a haze of smog covers the city. Four cities in China are on the ten worst cities for air pollution list. The Chinese government has been working hard to improve air pollution in Beijing before the Summer Olympics in 2008.

In London, people with weak lungs sometimes died when fog trapped smoke near the ground. In 1952 a very heavy London fog trapped large amounts of smoke over the city, and about four thousand people died. Thousands more became ill. Angry citizens demanded stronger laws to control air pollution.

Other countries also passed laws to control air pollution. The United States passed the Clean Air Act of 1970. This important law set limits on how much pollution could go into the air. Limits were set for common pollutants such as particles, sulfur dioxide, ozone, lead, nitrogen oxides, and carbon monoxide. Although air pollution travels across borders, countries have not been able to agree on international laws to control air pollution.

A couple walking in London in 1953 wear masks for protection against the smog on a foggy day.

FIGHTING PARTICLE POLLUTION

Thanks to clean air laws and new technology, European countries and the United States have greatly cut down the amount of particles going into the sky. In coal-burning power plants, a new process grinds the chunks of coal into fine dust before burning. This method creates more electricity from each ton of coal. So the power plants don't have to burn as much coal. In the smokestacks, the smoke passes through giant filters that catch most particles.

In central Europe in the 1950s, the beautiful Jizera Mountains and their valleys became known as the Black Triangle. The region is called a triangle because three countries, Germany, Poland, and the Czech Republic meet there. People called it black because of the terrible air pollution.

Ten large coal-burning power plants and other heavy industry burned 80 million tons (73 million metric tons) of coal per year, with little pollution control. Soot blackened the winter snow. Acid rain killed many of the spruce trees. Mountainsides had gray, dead trees instead of dark green forest. Most fish died in the forest streams.

Since 1990 the three countries sharing the Black Triangle have worked to control air pollution

GREENING THE BLACK FOREST

The pine trees of Germany's Black Forest were dying because of air pollution. The city of Freiburg switched to electric trains instead of cars. Air is cleaner in the forests around the city. People can enjoy a walk along the Rhine River under blue skies.

These trees in the Black Triangle in the Czech Republic were damaged by acid rain.

35

in the region. They modernized the power plants, making them grind coal to fine dust before burning it. The power plants also filter the smoke after burning. Scrubbers in the smokestacks catch even more small particles.

Snow stays white in the winter now in the Black Triangle. The forest has begun a slow recovery. With the rain less acidic, a few fish live in the forest streams.

However, many countries still have coal-burning power plants that don't use the new filters and other technology. Besides power plants, forest fires and other sources continue to send particles into the atmosphere. Around the world, much work still needs to be done to control particle pollution.

THE ROAD AHEAD

Because of stronger laws and new technology, many cities in Europe, Canada, and the United States have less smog than they did decades ago. In the United States, the total number of car miles driven has more than doubled since the 1960s. Yet, the total pollution from cars has dropped. Smaller, lighter cars with new engines get more miles per gallon, using less gasoline. The new engines

Cars are lined up during rush hour traffic in Los Angeles, California, in 2006. People in the United States drive more than they did in the 1960s, but air pollution has dropped.

have special devices that change most harmful gases in the exhaust into harmless ones before the exhaust goes into the air.

Even with these changes, cars are still an air pollution problem. In the United States, about half the air pollution comes from cars, trucks, buses, planes, and other vehicles. Anything that saves fuel or cuts down emissions from cars helps to improve air quality.

The Green Team, a group of students in Salt Lake City, Utah, is working to decrease the exhaust from cars in that city. There, winter smog has high levels of ozone and carbon monoxide. Students at Morningside Elementary School noticed the exhaust from idling buses and cars around their school. They started a Stop Idling! campaign. Kids wrote a song, sent lots of letters, talked to groups, and made bumper stickers.

The message to parents was to turn off their cars while waiting for their kids. The Green Team even got the

GET THE LEAD OUT!

Lead is a poisonous metal found naturally in the environment. It damages people's brains, blood, and other organs, and sickens plants. Lead used to be added to gasoline because it helped engines run better. But scientists found that car exhaust sent lots of tiny lead particles into the air. The lead poisoned people, animals, and plants.

The United States made leaded gasoline illegal. Afterward, the lead content in Americans' blood fell more than 80 percent. Doctors figure that the drop in lead pollution saves about twenty-two thousand lives a year in the United States. It also prevents countless other health problems. Most countries have banned leaded gasoline. Progress is slowest in African countries, but even there, more than half the gasoline sold is lead free.

school's bus policy changed. Bus drivers must turn off their buses while waiting for kids to get on. Exhaust no longer fills the air right when kids are getting out of school.

In 2006 the Green Team received the President's Environmental Youth Award. Many schools and cities around the country are starting Stop Idling campaigns of their own.

Americans alone could save 4 million gallons (more than 15 million liters) of gas every day by pumping up their tires. Keeping car tires at the correct air pressure improves gas mileage. (Gas mileage is how much gas it takes a particular car to drive a certain distance.) It not only saves money but it keeps extra carbon dioxide out of the air.

In Tampa, Florida, thirteen-year-old Savannah Walters started the Pump 'Em Up group. The group spreads the word about how much money—and oil—can be saved if people pump up their tire pressure to the right level. An organization called Action for Nature honored Savannah Walters as a 2006 Eco-Hero for her work. Her organization continues to be active.

TREES HELP THE FIGHT

Forests are sometimes called the lungs of Earth because trees put so much oxygen into the air. Trees also help to clean the air. Healthy trees absorb small particles and polluting gases out of the air. Every year, a mature tree soaks up 120 to 240 pounds (54 to 108 kilograms) of air pollution.

When Andy Lipkis was at summer camp as a boy, he learned that smog from Los Angeles was killing trees in

WHO'S PLANTING TREES IN YOUR CITY?

You can find out who is planting trees in your town or city at the website www.treelink.org. You can use the website to find out what kinds of trees grow well in your area and how to take care of them. There is also a kids' corner at www.treelink.org/kids.

the San Bernardino Mountains above the city. Adults at the camp told Andy that nothing could be done about the patches of dying pines and oaks. The single biggest cause of the smog was the endless row of cars zipping along the freeways below the tree line. And the cars were there to stay.

Andy couldn't stop thinking about the green forests that were turning into brown patches of dying trees. Several years later, when he was in college, Andy found that he could get low-cost seedlings of trees that could survive in smoggy air. These trees included incense cedars, Jeffrey pines, and sugar pines. But the job of planting the trees was far too big for one person.

Andy asked kids at his old summer camp to help. They were all eager to plant trees. Over the next few years, Andy and many others planted thousands of trees in the Los Angeles, California, area. They called themselves TreePeople. They also taught residents to water and care for the trees.

TreePeople started with a simple, powerful idea: plant a tree, and take care of it. In the early 1980s, TreePeople and the city of Los Angeles joined together to plant one million trees in Los Angeles in the four years before the 1984 Summer Olympics.

TreePeople founder Andy Lipkis is shown planting trees in Los Angeles in 2007. TreePeople members have been planting trees since the 1980s.

In 2006 TreePeople, schools, businesses, and the city of Los Angeles started work on planting another million trees. They focused on parts of the city they missed during the first Million Tree Campaign. Andy Lipkis was honored with the President's Call to Service Award in 2007. TreePeople continues its work and reports on projects on its organization's website.

CLEARING THE AIR IN CITIES

Other cities around the world are cleaning up air pollution in different ways. The world's top ten cities with the worst air pollution include four cities in China and four cities in India, along with Cairo, Egypt, and Jakarta, Indonesia.

Boys play cricket in thick smog in Calcutta, India, in 2006. Four cities in India are on the list of the cities with the worst air pollution in the world.

40

Women in Hong Kong, China, wear a mask or cover their mouth to protect against smog in 2004.

China has a population of 1.3 billion people—more people than any other country in the world. China's population and its industries are growing fast, and all that growth creates serious air pollution problems.

Coal and cars are both part of China's pollution problem. Coal is China's main source of power. But factory owners have not always used the best modern methods to prevent pollution from their coal-burning power plants. Already, China leads the world in putting sulfur dioxide in the air.

People wear face masks on the streets of many large Chinese cities. But masks can't keep all the pollution out of their lungs. Air pollution causes about three hundred thousand deaths every year in China. That number doesn't include deaths from smoking. In some Chinese cities, people have high levels of lead in their bodies, which can harm healthy brains. The lead comes from breathing in air polluted by coal-burning power plants and car exhaust.

42

The Chinese government ordered factories like this one in Beijing and surrounding areas to close during the 2008 Summer Olympics. The government also placed a limit on the number of cars allowed on the roads in the weeks before the games.

Chinese leaders are working to improve the country's air. The country has changed over to unleaded gasoline. New cars in China must meet the same pollution standards common in Europe and North America.

The Chinese people worked hard to improve the air quality in Beijing for the 2008 Olympic Games. The Olympics attract the world's top athletes and thousands of other people who watch the games. The Chinese wanted clean air for the athletes to breathe. They wanted their city to be at its best for the thousands of visitors. Cars and trucks were converted to run on natural gas, a cleaner fuel, instead of gasoline. New rules cut down the amount of driving in Beijing.

Many cities are working to keep the air clean by cutting back on car emissions. Around the world, buses, trains, and subways make it easy for people to get around in big cities. Special lanes or paths for bicycles, along with places to park bicycles, give people another clean way to travel. People walk more in cities that have parks, wide sidewalks, and lots of trees.

Some leaders have said that dirty air is the cost of modern life. But all around the world, other leaders have found ways to have clean air *and* modern life. These leaders say people have a right to clean air, just as much as they have a right to food, water, and a safe place to live.

Public transportation buses travel through Trafalgar Square in London in 2007. The city has increased the use of public transportation in recent years by charging a fee to drive cars in the central business district.

CHAPTER FOUR

CHOOSING CLEAN AIR

How do you fit in with protecting Earth's air quality? You can easily find out how clean or dirty the air is near your home and how that might affect you. You also can find out how you and your family affect air quality and if there's more you can do to help keep the air clean and healthy.

Our personal choices can affect air quality. But the search for air-friendly energy is a bigger issue that many scientists and others are working to solve. What kind of air quality will we have in the future? The choices that people and societies make in the present day will answer that question.

YOUR AIR QUALITY FORECAST

How clean is *your* air right now? Let's find out how you can check on your local air quality and compare it to air quality in other places.

In the United States, the Air Quality Index (AQI) tells how clean or dirty our air is and how the current air quality can affect our health. Many countries have similar air quality indexes. Scientists keep track of five major pollutants. They are ground-level ozone, particle pollution, carbon monoxide, sulfur dioxide, and nitrogen dioxide.

Scientists track air quality data with scientific instruments that are placed throughout the United States and gather data constantly. Scientists use this data to determine the Air Quality Index. The index rates air quality on a scale of 0 to 500. Scientists assign colors to show the level of health risk. The table on page 46 shows what the air quality levels are and what they mean.

AQI	Level of Health Concern	Cautionary Status
0 - 50	Good	**Green**. Little or no risk
51 - 100	Moderate	**Yellow**. Acceptable. Very sensitive people may have respiratory symptoms.
101 - 150	Unhealthful for sensitive groups	**Orange**. People in sensitive groups (those with lung disease and heart disease) may have health effects.
151 - 200	Unhealthy	**Red**. Everyone may begin to experience health effects, and people in sensitive groups may have more serious health effects.
201 - 300	Very unhealthy	**Purple**. Health alert: everyone may have more serious health effects.
301 - 500	Hazardous	**Maroon**. Health warnings: emergency conditions. Everyone is likely to be affected.

Source: EPA, AIRNow, at http://airnow.gov

In many countries, you can find out your air quality at a website. In the United States, you can get real-time air quality maps at www.airnow.gov. You can also get the air quality outlook. To check on air quality in Canada, go to www.cleanair.ca. For news on the air quality in London, go to the London Air Quality Network's website at www.londonair.org.uk. This website also links to air quality websites for the rest of the United Kingdom and Europe.

You can also check your local newspaper for the air quality forecast. It's probably on the weather page. Does your newspaper give you the UV Index?

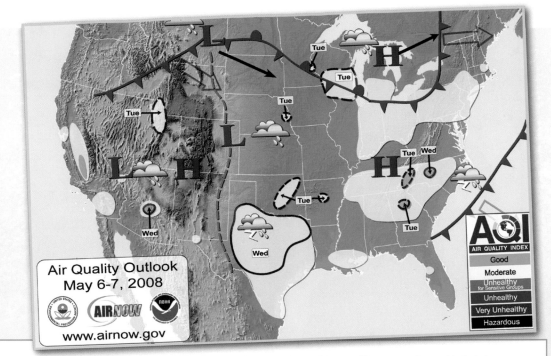

This map from www.airnow.gov shows what the air quality was like across the United States on May 6 and 7, 2008.

That's the ratings for ultraviolet radiation risk. What about pollen count? That's the measurement of the number of the grains of pollen in a certain amount of air.

NOW IT'S PERSONAL: TOBACCO FREE

People get sick from coal smoke, car exhaust, and smog. Tobacco smoke is just as bad for people's lungs as other kinds of smoke. It's almost like putting a factory smokestack into your mouth and breathing the smoke.

You can protect yourself from this personal form of air pollution by not smoking and by staying away from people who are smoking. In the United States,

Tobacco smoke is just as bad
for people's lungs as other kinds of smoke.

48

This girl in Bangladesh takes part in a campaign for Tobacco-Free Kids. Kids from all over the world can take part in events sponsored by the organization.

many young people first try smoking when they are in the sixth and seventh grades. People who get hooked on smoking are usually regular smokers by the time they're eighteen years old. Tobacco smoke begins to damage lungs in only a few months. Because of this, kids who smoke are worse at sports.

Most countries of the world have signed an international treaty to reduce tobacco use. They have taken actions such as raising taxes on tobacco and putting health warnings on cigarette packs. Many areas have also outlawed smoking in public places such as restaurants to protect people from secondhand smoke.

The best antismoking programs are run by kids, working closely with adults. That's because kids are the

KICK BUTTS DAY!

The biggest antismoking event of the year is Kick Butts Day! This annual event is sponsored by the Campaign for Tobacco-Free Kids and other groups. The date of each year's Kick Butts Day appears on the group's website www.tobaccofreekids.org. The website also has links to antismoking youth groups.

experts on how to reach other kids. Smoking among high school students went down by almost one-third in Ohio, Wisconsin, and New York schools after students led campaigns against smoking.

CARBON FOOTPRINTS

"Don't track that mud in the house!" Has your parent ever yelled at you for leaving dirty footprints on the living room carpet? When we put huge amounts of carbon dioxide, a greenhouse gas, into the air, we leave "dirty tracks" in the atmosphere. The measure of how much greenhouse gases you personally put into the air is called your carbon footprint. It is measured in units of carbon dioxide.

Burning fossil fuels makes up the largest part of humanity's carbon footprint. The size of the average carbon footprint for each person differs greatly among countries of the world. In countries with lots of cars, big houses, and electricity in every house, the average person puts lots of carbon dioxide in the air, just by going about daily life.

Forests and oceans absorb some carbon dioxide from the air and turn it into solid, living matter, such as tree trunks and algae. But science is finding that forests and

Big houses using lots of electricity mean that many people put pollution into the air without thinking about it.

COUNTING CARBON

How much carbon dioxide do you create in your daily life? You can find out online by answering some easy questions about your lifestyle. Check out the carbon calculator at www.carboncounter.org.

oceans can't absorb all the carbon dioxide that cars and power plants put into the air. The extra carbon dioxide adds to the problem of global warming.

Most countries in the world agree they should act to solve the problem. Government leaders are talking about new treaties agreeing to cut carbon emissions. They hope that all countries will sign up to do their part.

But people around the world aren't waiting for a new treaty. Lots of countries, cities, and even families are setting their own goals for making their carbon footprint smaller. The European Union, an economic and political group of European nations, has set a goal of cutting its energy use 20 percent by the year 2020. It also plans to get more of its energy from wind, solar, and other renewable energy sources. Renewable energy sources can be replaced fairly quickly and easily. If it achieves both goals, Europe will cut its output of carbon dioxide by almost one-third. In the United States, states such as California are also setting their own goals to cut pollution by greenhouse gases.

AIR-FRIENDLY ENERGY

Much of the air pollution you have learned about comes from power plants. Our modern cities and societies will continue to need lots of power, even if we all conserve energy. People are finding ways to create that power, without sending greenhouse gases into the sky.

People have used windmills for centuries to pump water from wells and to run flour mills. Modern wind turbines are much larger and more powerful than the older windmills. These new wind turbines stand on towers 200 feet (60 m) or more high. The giant blades spin in the wind. They are not much louder than the sound of the wind itself. The blades turn a shaft that changes the energy into electricity. The electricity flows down cables inside the tower. Wind farms have dozens or even hundreds of turbines. Electricity from all the turbines is collected in one spot and then sent out over the power lines, just like any other electricity.

One modern wind turbine can make enough electricity to power about six hundred homes. A wind farm can produce enough power for a small city. Unlike fossil fuels, wind power doesn't produce any carbon dioxide or greenhouse gases of any kind. Birds sometimes fly into the spinning blades and can be killed. But more birds die flying into buildings and power lines than die hitting wind turbines.

The electricity generated from wind power has more than tripled since 2000. It continues to grow fast. Germany leads the world in using wind power. The country

These windmills in Germany are in farmers' fields. Germany uses more wind power than any other country in the world.

These wind turbines are in a field of wheat in Kansas. Kansas is one of the U.S. states that is considered the best for wind power.

52

meets about 7 percent of its total energy needs through wind power. In the United States, the best states for wind power may be North Dakota, Kansas, Texas, Colorado, and Iowa. Ranchers could someday make as much money from selling wind energy as they do from their cattle and crops.

Solar energy has been around a long time too, ever since the first plant used sunlight as an energy

THAT'S THE SPIRIT!

In Iowa, students at Spirit Lake Community School District challenged their school superintendent, Harold Overman, to look for clean energy. Because the school sits on a high, windy ridge, it built two of its own wind turbines. These provide much of the district's electricity. Wind turbines cost money to build, but as soon as the blades started spinning, the school began to save money on electric bills. Money saved is going to sports teams, musical instruments, and science equipment. Plus the schools are keeping millions of pounds of carbon dioxide, sulfur dioxide, and other pollutants out of the air.

source. What's new, though, is that scientists are inventing ways to turn solar energy into electricity at a price people can afford. In countries like Japan and Germany, people are turning their roofs into small power plants. Solar cells are panels that use the sun's energy as a power source. People put solar cells on their roofs to turn sunlight into electricity for use in their homes. This form of solar energy doesn't create any smoke or greenhouse gases, and it doesn't even make a sound. Most people also keep their homes connected to the regular electric lines for power on cloudy days.

More people are using the sun's power to heat their water too. Water is pumped into solar panels, where sunlight heats the water. Then the water flows back into the house's water heater. In sunny countries like Israel and Spain, heating water with solar power is a great way to save money and help keep air clean.

This office building in Heidelberg, Germany, has solar cells on the roof to use the sun's energy to power the building.

BUILDING AN ATMOSPHERE

If air pollution got really bad, how hard would it be for scientists to build a healthy atmosphere without nature's help? Good question! In the 1990s, scientists in Arizona ran a real-life test to find the answer. They designed Biosphere 2 to be a small model of Biosphere 1—which is the Earth itself, and all the life on Earth. Billionaire Edward Bass funded the experiment.

Biosphere 2 was a 3.14-acre (1.27-hectare) building and science lab set up to be a closed ecosystem that supported itself. An ecosystem is a community of living things that depend on one another and their shared environment. Although Biosphere 2 was in the desert near Oracle, Arizona, it was sealed as tightly as a spaceship.

Biosphere 2, shown here in 1991, was in the desert in Arizona. Scientists sealed the complex as tightly as a spaceship. They wanted to see if they could run a biosphere as well as nature does.

This view from above Biosphere 2 shows the two dome-shaped buildings that balanced the air pressure in the ecosystems in Biosphere 2.

Biosphere 2 had different ecosystems, just like Earth does. These included a farm, tropics, a million-gallon (3.8 million-liter) "ocean," and a desert. Two large dome-shaped buildings acted as lungs to balance the air pressure. Scientists designed it to be a complete model Earth with balanced ecosystems that could make enough oxygen and food for eight people.

In 1991 eight scientists agreed to be sealed inside for two years. A ground crew outside Biosphere 2 always kept in touch with the eight men and women to be sure they were okay.

Although Biosphere 2 used the best science, the eight Biospherians inside ran into trouble. The oxygen level inside began to drop. The carbon dioxide level rose. Enough nitrous oxide built up that it affected the people's ability to think clearly. Some animal and plant species died out completely inside Biosphere 2. But the numbers of ants and cockroaches exploded. Algae matted the ocean.

Even though it had plants, Biosphere 2 failed to make enough oxygen for the people sealed inside. This woman was on the 1991–1993 team.

After a second mission failed to work any better, the Biosphere 2 missions stopped. A few years later, the owners sold Biosphere 2. The University of Arizona uses Biosphere 2 for research and education—but doesn't ask people to live sealed inside.

The lesson of Biosphere 2 is that scientists don't know how to build a healthy atmosphere that does all the things our Earth's atmosphere does for us. An old saying gives good advice about the atmosphere: "If you don't know how to fix something, don't break it!"

TOMORROW'S ATMOSPHERE

Our atmosphere has been amazingly tough. Even as people have poured smoke, new gases, and too much carbon dioxide into the air, it has managed to recover. Wind blows smoke away, rain washes soot out of the air, and oceans and forests absorb extra carbon dioxide. At the same time, the atmosphere keeps shielding us from harmful radiation.

But our atmosphere can't get rid of all the pollution on its own. All the dirty air makes one point perfectly clear: we need to put less pollution into the air. Scientists and engineers are finding ways to scrub particles out of smoke before it rises from smokestacks. They're also improving car engines so cars can go more miles on less fuel and so the gasoline that engines use burns cleaner.

But scientists can't clean up the air without our help. The fastest and cheapest way to improve air quality is for people to use less energy. We can all look at ways to make our carbon footprints smaller. The "Going Green" section of this book offers some ideas to help you get started.

The second-fastest way to improve air quality is to use energy sources that don't

57

SEND A REPORT TO THE WORLD

In the international Young Reporters for the Environment program, kids post articles and photos about the environment online. Over five hundred schools from fifteen countries are involved in this program run by the Foundation for Environmental Education. The site www.youngreporters.org has information on how schools can get involved.

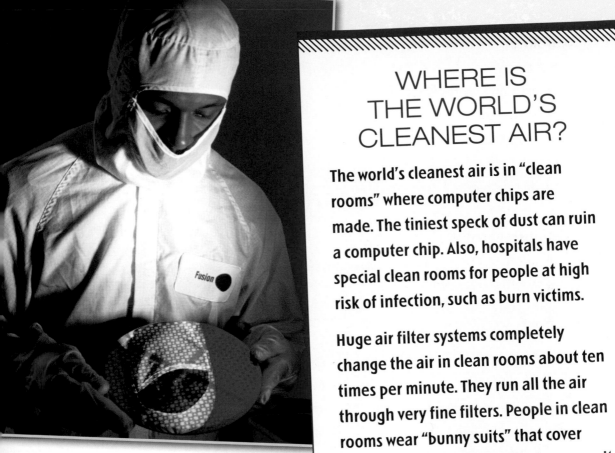

This technician is wearing a suit that keeps any stray hair or skin flakes from getting in the air as he works at a computer chip manufacturing plant.

WHERE IS THE WORLD'S CLEANEST AIR?

The world's cleanest air is in "clean rooms" where computer chips are made. The tiniest speck of dust can ruin a computer chip. Also, hospitals have special clean rooms for people at high risk of infection, such as burn victims.

Huge air filter systems completely change the air in clean rooms about ten times per minute. They run all the air through very fine filters. People in clean rooms wear "bunny suits" that cover them completely, almost like a spacesuit. These suits keep any stray hairs or skin flakes from getting in the air. A computer clean room has no more than one speck of dust per cubic foot (0.03 cu. m). That's about ten thousand times cleaner than a typical hospital operating room.

pollute. Wind energy, solar energy, and cars that use electricity as well as gas are all good ways to keep greenhouse gases out of the air. And burning less fossil fuel helps us keep the air clean.

In fact, people already are improving Earth's air quality. Since CFCs have been banned, the ozone layer is beginning to repair itself. Lots of the world's big cities, such as London and New York, have cleaner air than they had fifty years ago. Blades are spinning on new wind turbines in Oregon and California, sending clean energy into the power lines. Much work remains to be done, however, to protect Earth's air quality.

What will tomorrow's atmosphere be like? That's a question we can all help answer. Let's make it a clear blue sky.

New York City is just one of many of the world's largest cities that have improved air quality.

GOING GREEN

Lots of choices we make every day affect air quality—for better or worse. We'll breathe easier, in the present and the future, if we take action for better air quality. Here are some ideas to help you get started.

- **Walk or roll places.** Use your own body's power instead of a car to get places whenever you can. Walk or bike with friends to places near home. If it's too far to walk, share the ride. Carpool or take the bus with friends for trips farther away from home.

- **Check tire pressure.** Tell your parents they can save money on gas and cut back on gas emissions if the car's tire pressure is accurate. You can find out more at the Pump 'Em Up website www.pumpemup.org.

- **Buy food grown locally whenever possible.** Farmers' markets are often a good source. The fewer miles a tomato is trucked to the store, the less gasoline is burned and the fewer exhaust gases go into the air.

These students in the Philippines help plant trees along a highway to help fight pollution.

- **Plant trees.** And be sure to water them through the summer. Remember, trees and other green plants take in carbon dioxide that fossil fuels add to the air. Just one tree absorbs 2,000 pounds (900 kg) of CO_2 each year.

- **Avoid secondhand smoke whenever possible.** And don't start smoking in the first place.

- **Tell adults and other drivers to stop idling!** Ask a teacher if you can start a Stop Idling! campaign at your school. See the brochure at www .stopthesoot.org/idling_whats_the_problem.pdf for useful facts to help you get started.

ASK LEADERS TO CLEAR THE AIR

Kids can help pass tough air quality laws by sending their ideas to government leaders. Jolie Yang helped get the SmokeFreeOhio ballot measure passed in 2006 when she was a junior at Centerville High School in Ohio. The new law made workplaces in Ohio smoke free, including restaurants and bars. You can send elected officials e-mails or regular letters about your views on air pollution too. Not sure where to start? Look on the next page for a few helpful hints.

61

GOING GREEN

- **Tell your leaders what you think about air quality problems.** Your letter doesn't have to be long or complicated. Just explain how you feel, and use your own words.

- **Say exactly what you would like leaders to do.** For example, tell them if you think they should vote for or against laws for smoke-free workplaces, stronger controls on car emissions, and tough rules on air pollution.

- **In the United States, you can find the names of all elected officials at one website: www.usa.gov.** Click on "Contact elected officials" to find the senators and congressional representatives for your state. You can send an e-mail to elected officials directly from the website!

62

ENVIRONMENTAL GROUPS

Many environmental groups around the world are working to clean up the air. Here are just a few of the groups:

- **Clean Air Watch**
  http://www.cleanairwatch.org
  1250 Connecticut Ave. NW, Suite 200
  Washington, DC 20036
  202-558-3527

- **Earth 911**
  http://www.earth911.org
  Global Alerts, LLC.
  14646 N. Kierland Blvd.
  Scottsdale, AZ 85254
  480-889-2650

- **Environmental Defense**
  http://www.environmentaldefense.org
  257 Park Ave. South
  New York, NY 10010
  800-684-3322

- **Natural Resources Defense Council**
  http://www.nrdc.org
  In Spanish: http://www.nrdc.org/laondaverde
  40 West 20th St.
  New York, NY 10011
  212-727-2700

- **WWF International**
  http://www.wwf.org
  Av. du Mont Blanc 1196
  Gland
  Switzerland
  41 22 364 91 11

63

GLOSSARY

acid precipitation: rain, sleet, hail, or snow that falls from clouds polluted with acids

asthma: a lung disease that causes breathing problems. So far, there is no cure.

atmosphere: the layer of gases that surrounds Earth

atoms: tiny particles that are the building blocks of chemical elements

biosphere: all the life that exists in or on Earth's water, land, and sky

carbon cycle: the process by which carbon moves through the natural world

carbon dioxide (CO_2): a gas that is a mix of carbon and oxygen

carbon monoxide: a gas that is a mixture of carbon and oxygen. It is produced when fuel does not burn completely.

chlorofluorocarbons (CFCs): a group of human-made gases that include carbon, chlorine, fluorine, and other gases, used in the twentieth century in refrigerators and air conditioners

climate: usual weather patterns, or the typical weather in a specific region

fossil fuel: a fuel that formed underground from plants and animals that died millions of years ago

gas: a state of matter with no definite size or shape, not liquid or solid but a vapor

global warming: the gradual rising of Earth's temperature because of increased carbon dioxide and other heat-trapping gases in the atmosphere

greenhouse gases: a name for carbon dioxide and other gases that hold the sun's heat near Earth. Greenhouse gases cause global warming.

molecule: atoms joined by chemical bonds

nitrogen oxide: any of several gases made up of varying amounts of nitrogen and oxygen

ozone: a gas made up of three oxygen atoms

particle pollution: small particles found in the air, such as dust, smoke, ashes, and soot; can be from human sources or natural sources such as volcanoes

photosynthesis: the process by which plants use energy from the sun to convert carbon dioxide and water into sugar and oxygen

pollutant: a substance that makes the land, air, or water dirty

smog: a yellow or brown haze that forms when sunlight hits ground-level ozone and polluted air, changing the pollutants into new forms

sulfur dioxide: a toxic gas that is a mixture of sulfur and oxygen and is a major air pollutant. Sulfur is common in oil, coal, and common metals such as iron and aluminum.

wind turbine: a machine with big rotating blades that sit on top of a tower. The rotation of a turbine's blades turns wind energy into electrical power.

65

SELECTED BIBLIOGRAPHY

Allaby, Michael. *Air: The Nature of Atmosphere and the Climate.* New York: Facts on File, 1992.

Brown, Lester R. *Plan B 2.0: Rescuing a Planet under Stress and a Civilization in Trouble.* New York: W. W. Norton & Company, 2006.

Diamond, Jared. *Collapse: How Societies Choose to Fail or Succeed.* New York: Viking, 2005.

Graedel, Thomas E., and Paul J. Crutzen. *Atmosphere, Climate, and Change.* New York: Scientific American Library, 1997.

Lomborg, Bjorn. *The Skeptical Environmentalist: Measuring the Real State of the World.* Cambridge: Cambridge University Press, 2006.

Millennium Ecosystem Assessment. *Ecosystems and Human Well-Being: Synthesis.* Washington, DC: Island Press, 2005.

Science and Technology Department of the Carnegie Library of Pittsburgh. *The Handy Science Answer Book.* Farmington Hills, MI: Visible Ink Press, 1997.

Sherman, Joe. *Gasp! The Swift & Terrible Beauty of Air.* Washington, DC: Shoemaker & Hoard, 2004.

Suzuki, David, and Holly Dressel. *Good News for a Change: How Everyday People Are Helping the Planet.* Vancouver, BC: Greystone Books, 2002.

Suzuki, David, and Amanda McConnell. *The Sacred Balance: Rediscovering Our Place in Nature.* Vancouver, BC: Greystone Books, 2002.

Thomas, Lewis. *The Lives of a Cell: Notes of a Biology Watcher.* New York: Viking, 1974.

Trask, Crissy. *It's Easy Being Green: A Handbook for Earth-Friendly Living.* Salt Lake City: Gibbs Smith, 2006.

Wiland, Harry, Dale Bell, and Joseph D'Agnese. *Edens Lost & Found: How Ordinary Citizens Are Restoring Our Great Cities.* White River Junction, VT: Chelsea Green, 2006.

World Health Organization (WHO). Fact Sheets. 2006-2007. http://www.who.int/mediacentre/factsheets/ (May 7, 2008).

Worldwatch Institute. *2007 State of the World: Our Urban Future.* Washington, DC: Worldwatch Institute, 2007.

———. *Vital Signs 2006-2007: The Trends That Are Shaping Our Future.* Washington, DC: Worldwatch Institute, 2006.

WWF-World Wide Fund for Nature. *Living Planet Report 2006.* http://www.panda.org (May 7, 2008).

———. Add title. 2006. http://www.footprintnetwork.org/2006technotes (May 7, 2008).

67

FURTHER READING

Air Pollution—What's the Solution?
http://www.k12science.org/curriculum/airproj
This site offers an interactive and fun program on air quality, ozone, and particle pollution. Lessons are short and colorful, and links take users to more detailed information.

Change the World through Smart Shopping
http://www.ibuydifferent.org
It all adds up—the money that kids spend and the money parents spend to buy products their kids ask for. Take the shopping quiz and learn how you can make a difference by shopping green.

How Big Is Your Footprint?
http://www.ecofoot.org
Your use of fossil fuels, also known as your carbon footprint, plays a big part in setting the size of your ecological footprint, or the affects of your actions on the environment. This site offers an ecological footprint quiz in seven languages. You can find out what kind of footprint you and your family leave in the world and how you can make it smaller.

Johnson, Rebecca L. *Understanding Global Warming.* Minneapolis: Lerner Publications Company, 2009. Learn all about global warming and how it affects our planet.

Nagel, Shirley. *Tree Boy.* San Francisco: Sierra Club Books for Children, 1978. This book tells how teenager Andy Lipkis started his first campaigns to plant smog-resistant trees in the Los Angeles area.

NASA (National Aeronautics and Space Administration). *For Kids Only: Earth Science Enterprise*
http://kids.earth.nasa.gov/
This website provides kid-friendly information about how NASA studies land, air, water, and natural hazards and includes a glossary and teachers' guides.

Rupp, Rebecca. *Weather!* North Adams, MA: Storey Publishing, 2004. This lively book has great information about how weather works, plus projects such as how to start a tornado in a bottle or whip up a batch of atmosphere in the kitchen.

Silverstein, Alvin, Virginia Silverstein, and Laura Silverstein Nunn. *Weather and Climate.* Minneapolis: Twenty-First Century Books, 2008. This book presents almost everything you need to know about the weather and climate around the world.

Solutions Are in Our Nature!
http://www.davidsuzuki.org/kids
Dr. David Suzuki, a Canadian scientist, says, "Solutions are in our nature!" on his website for kids. The site has lots of ways that kids can help improve air quality, and it also includes homework help, games, activities, and puzzles about the environment. Links lead to other fun science websites.

Suzuki, David, and Kathy Vanderlinden. *Eco-Fun: Great Projects, Experiments, and Games for a Greener Earth.* Vancouver, BC: Greystone Books, 2003. This book includes many great hands-on activities that help kids learn about keeping our planet green.

Vogt, Gregory. *The Atmosphere: Planetary Heat Engine.* Minneapolis: Twenty-First Century Books, 2007. This book presents facts about Earth's atmosphere and how it affects our lives.

Welsbacher, Anne. *Protecting Earth's Rain Forests.* Minneapolis: Lerner Publications Company, 2009. Read all about Earth's rain forests and how we can help protect them.

What's Up in the Air Today?
http://www.epa.gov/kids/air.htm
The U.S. government's main agency on air quality, the EPA, has air quality chameleons and Dusty the asthma goldfish on their kids' website. Parts of the site are in Spanish. The site also has a list of teaching resources on air.

INDEX

71

ABOUT THE AUTHOR

Valerie Rapp writes about how nature works, how people connect to nature, and how we're going to survive in the twenty-first century. She is the author of four books and many scientific publications. One of her previous books, *Life in a River,* was a finalist for the 2003 Oregon Book Award in Children's Literature. She and her husband have lived for many years in a log home in the Oregon mountains.

PHOTO ACKNOWLEDGMENTS

The images in this book are used with the permission of: © iStockphoto.com/Volker Kreinacke, pp. all backgrounds, 1 (left), 3 (top); © Photodisc/Getty Images, pp. all backgrounds, 1 (right), 4 (right), 5, 19, 24; © iStockphoto.com/Richard Schmidt-Zuper, p. 3 (middle); © age fotostock/SuperStock, pp. 3 (bottom), 6, 58; NASA, pp. 4-5, 13; © iStockphoto.com/Nicole S. Young, p. 4 (left); © Martin Bernetti/AFP/Getty Images, p. 7; © Royalty-Free/CORBIS, p.8; © Bill Hauser/Independent Picture Service, pp. 9, 10, 12, 15, 29; © iStockphoto.com/Eric Isselée, p. 14; © Vin Morgan/AFP/Getty Images, p. 16; © Jon Love/Riser/Getty Images, p. 17 (left); © iStockphoto.com/Midhat Becar, p. 17 (right); © Samantha Sin/AFP/Getty Images, p. 18; © The Print Collector/Alamy, p. 20; © Sergio Dorantes/CORBIS, p. 21; AP Photo/Jonathan Head, p. 22; © iStockphoto.com/YinYang, p. 23; © iStockphoto.com/Daniel Stein, p. 26; © China Photos/Getty Images, p. 33; © Monty Fresco/Topical Press Agency/Getty Images, p. 34; © Tom Stoddart/Hulton Archive/Getty Images, p. 35; © David McNew/Getty Images, p. 36; © iStockphoto.com/Marek Uliasz, p. 37; © iStockphoto.com/Christine Balderas, p. 38; © Charley Gallay/Getty Images, p. 39; AP Photo/Sucheta Das, p. 40; © Mike Clarke/AFP/Getty Images, p. 41; © Guang Niu/Getty Images, p. 42; © Tim Graham/Tim Graham Photo Library/Getty Images, p. 43; © Rubens Abboud/Alamy, p. 45 (main); © Lori Adamski Peek/Stone/Getty Images, p. 45 (inset); AIRNow, www.airnow.gov, p. 47; © Jewel Samad/AFP/Getty Images, p. 48; © iStockphoto.com/Harry Hu, p. 49; © iStockphoto.com/Yunus Arakon, p. 50; © Norbert Rosing/National Geographic/Getty Images, p. 51; © Altrendo Images/Altrendo/Getty Images, p. 52; © Edward Parker/Alamy, p. 53; AP Photo, p. 54; © Visions of America, LLC/Alamy, p. 55; AP Photo/Jeff Robbins, p. 56; © Frans Lemmens/Photographer's Choice/Getty Images, p. 59; © Wang Leng/Asia Images/Getty Images, p. 60; AP Photo/Bullit Marquez, p. 61.

Front Cover: © iStockphoto.com/Volker Kreinacke (wind turbines); © Photodisc/Getty Images (background, title, spine); © VisionsofAmerica/Joe Sohm/The Image Bank/Getty Images (middle left); © Stuart O'Sullivan/Taxi/Getty Images (middle right).

Back Cover: © iStockphoto.com/Volker Kreinacke; © Photodisc/Getty Images.